January

New Beginnings

"Every moment is a fresh beginning." – T.S. Eliot

January 1st

Affirmation:

I embrace the new year with open arms, ready to create the life I desire.

365 Days of Positivity Quotes

Asha

Published by Asha, 2024.

While every precaution has been taken in the preparation of this book, the publisher assumes no responsibility for errors or omissions, or for damages resulting from the use of the information contained herein.

365 DAYS OF POSITIVITY QUOTES

First edition. November 21, 2024.

ISBN: 979-8230624752

Written by Asha.

January 2nd

Affirmation:

I trust the process and embrace the unknown.

January 3rd
Affirmation:

I am capable of achieving anything I set my mind to.

January 4th
Affirmation:
Today, I choose to be happy and content.

January 5th
Affirmation
I attract positivity and good energy into my life.

January 6th

Affirmation

I release what no longer serves me and make room for growth.

January 7th
Affirmation
I am becoming the best version of myself every day.

January 8th
Affirmation
I deserve the success and abundance that comes my way.

January 9th

Affirmation

I am proud of how far I've come and excited about where I'm going.

January 10th

Affirmation

I let go of fear and embrace the future with confidence.

January 11th

Affirmation

I am grateful for every lesson, even the difficult ones.

January 12th

Affirmation

I am worthy of love, respect, and compassion.

January 13th

Affirmation

I have the power to shape my reality.

January 14th
Affirmation
I am enough just as I am.

January 15th
Affirmation
My potential is limitless.

January 16th
Affirmation
I am resilient, strong, and brave.

January 17th

Affirmation

I trust that everything in my life is unfolding perfectly.

January 18th
Affirmation
I honor my progress, no matter how small.

January 19th

Affirmation

I embrace challenges as opportunities for growth.

January 20th
Affirmation
I am surrounded by love and abundance.

January 21st
Affirmation
I am worthy of my dreams.

January 22nd
Affirmation
I choose peace over worry.

January 23rd
Affirmation
I have the courage to pursue my goals.

January 24th
Affirmation
I am a magnet for success.

January 25th

Affirmation

I am in control of my thoughts, feelings, and actions.

January 26ᵗʰ
Affirmation
I deserve to take up space and speak my truth.

January 27th
Affirmation
I believe in my abilities and trust my intuition.

January 28th
Affirmation
I am learning, growing, and becoming better each day.

January 29th

Affirmation

I release the need for perfection and celebrate progress.

January 30th

Affirmation

I am filled with optimism and excitement for all the possibilities this year holds.

January 31st
Affirmation
I am in tune with my inner self and honor my needs.

February

Self-Love & Compassion

"You yourself, as much as anybody in the entire universe, deserve your love and affection."

— Buddha

February 1st

Affirmation

I choose to love myself unconditionally.

February 2nd

Affirmation

I am deserving of self-compassion and care.

February 3rd
Affirmation
I treat myself with kindness and understanding.

February 4th
Affirmation
I release negative self-talk and replace it with positive affirmations.

February 5th
Affirmation
I am proud of who I am becoming.

February 6th
Affirmation
My flaws make me unique and beautiful.

February 7th
Affirmation
I radiate confidence, self-respect, and inner harmony.

February 8th
Affirmation
I am worthy of the same love and care I give to others.

February 8th

Affirmation

I choose to nourish my mind, body, and soul.

February 9th

Affirmation

I am the architect of my life, and I build it with love.

February 10th

Affirmation

I forgive myself for past mistakes and release guilt.

February 11th

Affirmation

I honor my boundaries and protect my energy.

February 12th

Affirmation

I am patient with myself as I grow and evolve.

February 13th
Affirmation
I trust in the timing of my life.

February 14th
Affirmation
I am worthy of all the good things that come my way.

February 15th

Affirmation

I am a source of love and light in the world.

February 16th
Affirmation
I love and accept myself exactly as I am.

February 17th

Affirmation

I am enough just as I am in this moment.

February 18th

Affirmation

I deserve to take care of myself.

February 19th

Affirmation

I choose to focus on what I can control and let go of what I cannot.

February 20th

Affirmation

I am a priority in my own life.

February 21st
Affirmation
I believe in myself and my abilities.

February 22nd
Affirmation
I am deserving of the love I give to others.

February 23rd
Affirmation
My happiness comes from within.

February 24th
Affirmation
I celebrate my uniqueness and honor my individuality.

February 25th

Affirmation

I am constantly growing and evolving into a better version of myself.

February 26th
Affirmation
I am kind, compassionate, and loving towards myself.

February 27th

Affirmation

I am allowed to set boundaries and say no when I need to.

February 28th
Affirmation
I am worthy of love, kindness, and respect, starting with how I treat myself.

March
Growth & Resilience

"The oak fought the wind and was broken,
the willow bent when it must and survived."
— Robert Jordan

March 1ˢᵗ

Affirmation

I am stronger than I think, and I can handle anything that comes my way.

March 2nd
Affirmation
I embrace change as an opportunity for growth.

March 3rd

Affirmation

I am resilient and rise stronger from every challenge.

March 4th

Affirmation

I have the power to turn obstacles into opportunities.

March 5th

Affirmation

I trust my journey, even when it's difficult.

March 6th

Affirmation

I am in control of my thoughts and reactions.

March 7th
Affirmation
I release what no longer serves my highest good.

March 8th

Affirmation

I am committed to my personal growth.

March 9th

Affirmation

I grow stronger with every experience.

March 9th

Affirmation

I grow stronger with every experience.

March 10th

Affirmation

I face challenges with courage and determination.

March 11th

Affirmation

I trust myself to make the best decisions for my life.

March 12th
Affirmation
I am constantly learning and improving.

March 13th

Affirmation

I embrace discomfort as a sign of growth.

March 14th

Affirmation

I rise above adversity and emerge stronger than before.

March 15th

Affirmation

I have the power to overcome anything.

March 16th

Affirmation

I trust that setbacks are setups for future success.

March 17th
Affirmation
I am in charge of my own happiness.

March 18th

Affirmation

I have the courage to keep going, no matter what.

March 19th

Affirmation

I am proud of my resilience and strength.

March 20th

Affirmation

I embrace life's challenges with a positive mindset.

March 21st

Affirmation

I trust myself to navigate through difficult times.

March 22nd
Affirmation
I have the power to rewrite my story at any moment.

March 23rd
Affirmation
I welcome growth and transformation into my life.

March 24th
Affirmation
I trust that everything happens for a reason.

March 25th

Affirmation

I am patient with myself and my journey.

March 26th
Affirmation
I have the ability to overcome fear and doubt.

March 27th
Affirmation
I am adaptable and open to change.

March 28th

Affirmation

I believe in my ability to create positive change.

March 29th
Affirmation
I am capable of achieving greatness through perseverance.

March 30th
Affirmation
I embrace challenges as stepping stones to success.

March 31st

Affirmation

I am resilient and capable of overcoming any challenge that comes my way.

April
Positivity & Gratitude

"Wear gratitude like a cloak, and it will feed

every corner of your life."

— Rumi

April 1st

Affirmation

I choose to focus on the good in every situation.

April 2nd

Affirmation
I am grateful for all the blessings in my life.

April 3rd
Affirmation
I find joy in the present moment.

April 4th
Affirmation
I am surrounded by positive energy.

April 5th
Affirmation
I attract positive experiences into my life.

April 6th
Affirmation
I am thankful for the abundance that flows into my life.

April 7th
Affirmation
I choose to see the beauty in every day.

April 8th
Affirmation
I am grateful for the lessons I've learned from every challenge.

April 9th
Affirmation
I embrace each day with a grateful heart.

April 10th

Affirmation

I radiate positivity and attract it back into my life.

April 11th
Affirmation
I appreciate the small joys life offers.

April 12th
Affirmation
I am thankful for the love and support I receive from others.

April 13th

Affirmation

I choose to be grateful even in difficult times.

April 14th
Affirmation
I focus on the blessings, not the hardships.

April 15th
Affirmation

I am a magnet for positivity and good energy.

April 16th

Affirmation

I celebrate the little victories in life.

April 17th

Affirmation

I am grateful for the people who uplift and support me.

April 18th

Affirmation

I practice gratitude daily and it transforms my life.

April 19th
Affirmation
I am thankful for today's opportunities and possibilities.

April 20th

Affirmation

I appreciate the beauty that surrounds me.

April 21st
Affirmation

I choose to be thankful for everything I have.

April 22nd
Affirmation
My heart is full of gratitude and positivity.

April 23rd

Affirmation

I focus on the present and find joy in simple moments.

April 24th

Affirmation

I am grateful for all the opportunities that come my way.

April 25th
Affirmation
I appreciate every blessing, no matter how small.

April 26th
Affirmation
I embrace each moment with a sense of gratitude.

April 27th
Affirmation
I choose to see life through a lens of positivity.

April 28th
Affirmation
I am thankful for the gift of another day.

April 29th

Affirmation

I embrace new beginnings with excitement and confidence, knowing they lead to growth.

April 30th

Affirmation

I trust the process of life and welcome the opportunities that each new day brings.

May

Confidence & Courage

"You gain strength, courage, and confidence by every experience in which you really stop to look fear in the face."
— Eleanor Roosevelt

May 1st

Affirmation

I am confident in my abilities and trust myself completely.

May 2nd

Affirmation

I am brave, bold, and confident in all that I do.

May 3rd
Affirmation
I trust myself to handle anything that comes my way.

May 4th

Affirmation

I believe in my unique abilities and talents.

May 5th
Affirmation
I have the courage to step outside of my comfort zone.

May 6th
Affirmation
I embrace every opportunity with confidence and excitement.

May 7th
Affirmation
I am confident in my ability to achieve my goals.

May 8th

Affirmation

I trust that I have the strength to succeed.

May 9th
Affirmation
I am worthy of the goals and dreams I pursue.

May 10th
Affirmation
I am fearless in the pursuit of what sets my soul on fire.

May 11th
Affirmation
I have the confidence to be my true self.

May 12th

Affirmation

I embrace my individuality and shine brightly.

May 13th

Affirmation

I am deserving of success and happiness.

May 14th
Affirmation
I have the power to create the life I desire.

May 15th
Affirmation
I trust my inner wisdom to guide me.

May 16th
Affirmation
I am confident in my decisions and trust my instincts.

May 17th
Affirmation
I am not afraid to take risks and embrace new opportunities.

May 18th
Affirmation
I have everything I need within me to succeed.

May 19th
Affirmation
I believe in myself and my ability to make things happen.

May 20th

Affirmation

I am strong, capable, and confident in all that I do.

May 21st
Affirmation
I am proud of who I am becoming.

May 22nd

Affirmation

I am brave enough to chase my dreams.

May 23rd
Affirmation
I am confident in my ability to create positive change.

May 24th
Affirmation
I trust myself to make the best choices for my future.

May 25th
Affirmation
I have the power to overcome any fear or doubt.

May 26th
Affirmation
I believe in my ability to achieve great things.

May 27th

Affirmation

I am confident in my ability to navigate through life's challenges.

May 28th

Affirmation

I embrace uncertainty with courage and confidence.

May 29th
Affirmation
I have the strength to take bold steps toward my goals.

May 30th

Affirmation

I am confident in my ability to create a fulfilling life.

May 30th

Affirmation

I am confident in my ability to create a fulfilling life.

May 31ˢᵗ
Affirmation
I am worthy of the success I seek.

June
Inner Peace & Mindfulness

"Peace comes from within. Do not seek it without."
— Buddha

June 1st

Affirmation
I am calm, centered, and grounded.

June 2nd
Affirmation
I find peace in the present moment.

June 3rd

Affirmation

I choose to release all tension and stress.

June 4th
Affirmation
I am in control of my thoughts and choose peace.

June 5th
Affirmation
I am worthy of inner peace and tranquility.

June 6th
Affirmation
I embrace stillness and allow myself to be at peace.

June 7th
Affirmation
I find joy in the simple moments of life.

June 8th

Affirmation

I release worry and choose to live with calm and clarity.

June 9th
Affirmation
I am in harmony with my surroundings.

June 10th
Affirmation
I breathe deeply and release all worries.

June 11th

Affirmation

I am fully present in every moment.

June 12th

Affirmation

I allow myself to rest and recharge when needed.

June 13th
Affirmation
I choose to cultivate peace within my mind and body.

June 14th
Affirmation
I find peace in letting go of what I cannot control.

June 15th
Affirmation
I create space for stillness and reflection in my life.

June 16th
Affirmation
I embrace moments of quiet as opportunities for growth.

June 17th
Affirmation
I am at peace with my past, present, and future.

June 18th

Affirmation

I find inner peace through acceptance and gratitude.

June 19th
Affirmation
I trust that everything is unfolding as it should.

June 20th
Affirmation
I am patient with myself and the journey I am on.

June 21st

Affirmation

I approach life with grace, ease, and calm.

June 22nd
Affirmation
I release all negativity and choose peace over worry.

June 23rd
Affirmation
I am in alignment with my inner self and trust my path.

June 24th
Affirmation
I remain calm and collected in all situations.

June 25th

Affirmation

I am at peace with who I am and where I am in life.

June 26th
Affirmation
I find peace in embracing uncertainty and change.

June 27th

Affirmation

I am grounded in the present moment, free from worry.

June 28th
Affirmation
I choose to let go of the things that no longer serve me.

June 29th
Affirmation
I create a life of peace, joy, and fulfillment.

June 30th

Affirmation

I nurture my soul with peaceful thoughts and actions.

July

Motivation & Action

"The future depends on what you do today."

— Mahatma Gandhi

July 1ˢᵗ

Affirmation

I am motivated, energized, and ready to achieve my goals.

July 2nd
Affirmation
I take action every day towards my dreams.

July 3rd
Affirmation
I am committed to making my vision a reality.

July 4th

Affirmation

I am full of energy and excited about life's opportunities.

July 5th

Affirmation

I take bold, courageous steps toward success.

July 6th
Affirmation
I trust in my ability to achieve greatness.

July 7th

Affirmation

I am proactive and take responsibility for my happiness.

July 8th

Affirmation

I create opportunities for success through focused action.

July 9th

Affirmation

I am motivated to keep pushing forward, even when it's hard.

July 10th
Affirmation
I am in control of my destiny and take charge of my future.

July 11th

Affirmation

I have the energy, passion, and drive to achieve my dreams.

July 12th
Affirmation
I am focused, determined, and ready for success.

July 13th
Affirmation
I turn obstacles into opportunities with my mindset.

July 14th
Affirmation
I am a person of action and get things done.

July 15th

Affirmation

I take the necessary steps today to create the life I want.

July 16th
Affirmation
I believe in my ability to make things happen.

July 17th
Affirmation
I trust in my capacity to overcome challenges.

July 18th
Affirmation
I make progress every day, no matter how small.

July 19th
Affirmation
I am driven by passion, purpose, and my goals.

July 20th

Affirmation

I embrace challenges as opportunities for growth and learning.

July 21st

Affirmation

I stay motivated by focusing on my "why."

July 22nd
Affirmation
I am unstoppable in the pursuit of my dreams.

July 23rd
Affirmation
I turn my ideas into reality through focused action.

July 24th
Affirmation
I trust that my hard work will pay off in the end.

July 25th
Affirmation
I am constantly moving forward toward my dreams.

July 26th
Affirmation
I act with confidence, courage, and purpose.

July 27th

Affirmation

I am resilient and refuse to give up on my goals.

July 28th
Affirmation
I stay focused on what matters most to me.

July 29th
Affirmation
I have the power to create change through action.

July 30th
Affirmation
I wake up every day excited and motivated to pursue my dreams.

July 31st
Affirmation
I am filled with motivation and take bold steps toward achieving my goals today.

August
Health & Wellness

"Take care of your body. It's the only place
you have to live."
— Jim Rohn

August 1ˢᵗ
Affirmation
I prioritize my health and well-being.

August 2nd
Affirmation
I nourish my body with healthy choices.

August 3rd
Affirmation
I am in tune with my body's needs and honor them.

August 4th
Affirmation
I am strong, healthy, and full of energy.

August 5th
Affirmation
I choose foods that nourish and energize me.

August 6th

Affirmation

I move my body every day to stay strong and healthy.

August 7th
Affirmation
I am grateful for my body and all it does for me.

August 8th

Affirmation

I choose wellness and vitality in every area of my life.

August 9th
Affirmation
I am committed to living a healthy, balanced life.

August 10th

Affirmation

I listen to my body and give it what it needs to thrive.

August 11th
Affirmation
I care for my mind, body, and spirit every day.

August 12th

Affirmation

I release habits that no longer serve my health and well-being.

August 12th

Affirmation

I am worthy of self-care and prioritize it daily.

August 13th
Affirmation
I am dedicated to becoming the healthiest version of myself.

August 14th

Affirmation

I choose to focus on what makes me feel good and vibrant.

August 15th
Affirmation
I treat my body with kindness and respect.

August 16th

Affirmation

I honor my body by giving it proper rest and care.

August 17th
Affirmation
I release stress and embrace peace and relaxation.

August 18th

Affirmation

I make healthy choices that support my long-term well-being.

August 19th

Affirmation

I love my body and treat it with the care it deserves.

August 20th
Affirmation
I make time to move my body in ways that feel good.

August 21st
Affirmation
I am constantly improving my health and vitality.

August 22nd
Affirmation
I choose to live a life full of health, happiness, and energy.

August 23rd
Affirmation
I balance rest and activity to maintain my well-being.

August 24th
Affirmation
I am grateful for my strong and capable body.

August 25th
Affirmation
I listen to my body's signals and honor them.

August 26th
Affirmation
I am full of life, energy, and vitality.

August 27th
Affirmation
I create space for rest, relaxation, and rejuvenation.

August 28th
Affirmation
I make time for self-care because I deserve it.

August 29th

Affirmation

I am in control of my health and well-being.

August 30th

Affirmation

I embrace each day with vitality, nourishing my body, mind, and spirit with positive choices.

August 31st

Affirmation:

I trust in my ability to adapt, grow, and thrive through every season of life.

September
Creativity & Innovation
"Creativity is intelligence having fun."
— Albert Einstein

September 1st

Affirmation:

I am creative and full of new ideas.

September 2nd
Affirmation:
I embrace my unique creative expression.

September 3rd
Affirmation:
I am constantly learning and growing creatively.

September 4th

Affirmation:

I trust my creative process and intuition.

September 5ᵗʰ

Affirmation:

I allow myself to think outside the box.

September 6th
Affirmation:
I create with passion, purpose, and joy.

September 7th
Affirmation:
I am confident in my ability to find creative solutions.

September 8th
Affirmation:
I embrace new challenges with a creative mindset.

September 9th

Affirmation:

I am a source of inspiration and innovation.

September 10th

Affirmation:
I give myself permission to explore new ideas.

September 11th
Affirmation:
I am constantly expanding my creative potential.

September 12th
Affirmation:
I approach every situation with a creative perspective.

September 12th
Affirmation:
I have the power to bring my ideas to life.

September 13th

Affirmation:

I am excited about all the creative possibilities in my life.

September 14th
Affirmation:
I find inspiration in the world around me.

September 15th

Affirmation:

I trust my ability to come up with brilliant ideas.

September 16th
Affirmation:
I am always learning, growing, and improving my craft.

September 17th

Affirmation:

I am proud of my unique creative expression.

September 18th
Affirmation:
I give myself the freedom to explore and create.

September 19th
Affirmation:
I trust the process of creativity and innovation.

September 20th

Affirmation:

I am a creative problem-solver and find joy in innovation.

September 21st

Affirmation:

I am open to creative inspiration from unexpected sources.

September 22nd
Affirmation:
I am confident in sharing my creative gifts with the world.

September 23rd
Affirmation:
I am constantly expanding my creative abilities.

September 24th
Affirmation:
I allow myself to be curious, playful, and imaginative.

September 25th
Affirmation:
I trust that my creativity will lead me to new opportunities.

September 26th
Affirmation:
I embrace the creative process and let it unfold naturally.

September 27th
Affirmation:
I am a magnet for creative inspiration and ideas.

September 28th

Affirmation:

I embrace my unique creativity and allow it to flow freely in all areas of my life.

September 29th

Affirmation:

I am a source of inspiration and originality, and I share my unique perspective with the world.

September 30th
Affirmation:
My imagination knows no bounds, and I explore it with joy and enthusiasm.

October

Love & Relationships

"The best thing to hold onto in life is each other."

— Audrey Hepburn

October 1st

Affirmation:

I attract loving and healthy relationships.

October 2nd

Affirmation:

I am worthy of love and affection.

October 3rd
Affirmation:
I give and receive love freely and openly.

October 4th
Affirmation:
I nurture my relationships with care and kindness.

October 5th

Affirmation:

I am surrounded by love and positivity.

October 6th

Affirmation:

I communicate openly and honestly in my relationships.

October 7th
Affirmation:
I am grateful for the love and connection in my life.

October 8th

Affirmation:

I deserve relationships that are based on trust and respect.

October 9th

Affirmation:

I choose to surround myself with loving and supportive people.

October 10th
Affirmation:
I am worthy of deep and meaningful connections.

October 11th
Affirmation:
I attract love, joy, and peace into my relationships.

October 12th

Affirmation:

I nurture the love I have for myself and others.

October 13th
Affirmation:
I give love freely without expectation or attachment.

October 14th
Affirmation:
I deserve to be loved for who I am.

October 15th

Affirmation:

I attract relationships that bring out the best in me.

October 16th

Affirmation:

I trust that love flows into my life effortlessly.

October 17th

Affirmation:

I am a source of love, compassion, and kindness.

October 18th
Affirmation:
I create harmonious and loving relationships.

October 19th

Affirmation:

I am open to receiving love in all forms.

October 20th
Affirmation:
I am worthy of love, joy, and connection.

October 21st

Affirmation:

I honor the love I have for myself and others.

October 22nd
Affirmation:
I attract relationships that are healthy and fulfilling.

October 23rd

Affirmation:

I am deserving of love, respect, and loyalty.

October 24th

Affirmation:

I radiate love and attract it back to me.

October 25th
Affirmation:
I give and receive love unconditionally.

October 26th

Affirmation:

I nurture my relationships with love, patience, and understanding.

October 27th

Affirmation:

I attract loving and caring relationships into my life.

October 28th
Affirmation:
I deserve relationships filled with love, laughter, and joy.

October 29th

Affirmation:

I trust that love flows into my life naturally.

October 30th
Affirmation:
I am a magnet for loving, supportive, and joyful relationships.

October 31st

Affirmation:

I open my heart to love and meaningful connections, attracting positive energy into my relationships.

November

Success & Abundance

"Success is not the key to happiness. Happiness is the key to success. If you love what you are doing, you will be successful."

— Albert Schweitzer

November 1st

Affirmation:

I am deserving of success and abundance in my life.

November 2nd
Affirmation:
I am a magnet for wealth, success, and prosperity.

November 3rd
Affirmation:
I attract opportunities for growth, success, and abundance.

November 4th

Affirmation:

I am open to receiving all the abundance life has to offer.

November 5th

Affirmation:

I am worthy of the wealth and success that flows into my life.

November 6th

Affirmation:

I trust that abundance flows into my life effortlessly.

November 7th
Affirmation:
I am grateful for the abundance that surrounds me.

November 8th
Affirmation:
I create success through hard work and determination.

November 9th

Affirmation:

I attract opportunities that align with my goals and dreams.

November 10th
Affirmation:
I deserve to live a life of abundance and prosperity.

November 11th

Affirmation:

I am worthy of achieving great things in life.

November 12th

Affirmation:

I am open to receiving financial abundance and security.

November 13th
Affirmation:
I am successful in everything I do.

November 14th
Affirmation:
I trust that success is flowing into my life.

November 15th

Affirmation:

I attract opportunities that allow me to grow and prosper.

November 16th
Affirmation:
I am aligned with the energy of abundance and success.

November 17th

Affirmation:

I am grateful for the financial abundance in my life.

November 18th
Affirmation:
I am worthy of achieving my goals and dreams.

November 19th

Affirmation:

I trust that I am on the path to success and abundance.

November 20th
Affirmation:
I am open to receiving all forms of prosperity and wealth.

November 21st

Affirmation:

I create wealth and success through hard work and dedication.

November 22nd

Affirmation:

I am deserving of the success and abundance that flows to me.

November 23rd

Affirmation:

I am constantly attracting new opportunities for success.

November 24th

Affirmation:

I believe in my ability to create wealth and abundance.

November 25th
Affirmation:
I am aligned with the energy of abundance and prosperity.

November 26th

Affirmation:

I trust that I am always supported in my journey to success.

November 27th
Affirmation:
I am worthy of living a life filled with abundance and joy.

November 28th

Affirmation:

I attract opportunities for success and financial growth.

November 29th

Affirmation:

I am open to receiving all the success and abundance the universe has to offer.

November 30th

Affirmation:

I am constantly creating new opportunities for success and prosperity.

December
Gratitude & Reflection

"Gratitude turns what we have into enough."
— Aesop

December 1st
Affirmation:
I am grateful for all the blessings in my life.

December 2nd

Affirmation:

I reflect on the past year with gratitude and grace.

December 3rd
Affirmation:
I am thankful for the lessons I have learned this year.

December 4th
Affirmation:
I choose to focus on all the good in my life.

December 5th

Affirmation:

I am grateful for the people who support and uplift me.

December 6th

Affirmation:

I acknowledge and appreciate all my accomplishments this year.

December 7th
Affirmation:
I am thankful for the growth I have experienced this year.

December 8th

Affirmation:

I reflect on the challenges I faced with gratitude for the lessons.

December 9th

Affirmation:

I am grateful for the abundance that surrounds me.

December 10th
Affirmation:
I embrace the new year with gratitude and hope.

December 11th

Affirmation:

I am thankful for the love and joy in my life.

December 12th

Affirmation:

I am grateful for the opportunities that have come my way.

December 13th

Affirmation:

I choose to end this year with a heart full of gratitude.

December 14th
Affirmation:
I am thankful for the journey and the lessons it has brought me.

December 15th
Affirmation:
I am grateful for the strength and resilience I have shown this year.

December 16th
Affirmation:
I reflect on this year with love and appreciation.

December 17th
Affirmation:
I am thankful for the support and love I have received.

December 18th

Affirmation:

I am grateful for the experiences that have shaped me this year.

December 19th

Affirmation:

I choose to move into the new year with a heart full of gratitude.

December 20th

Affirmation:

I am thankful for all the ways I have grown and evolved this year.

December 21ˢᵗ

Affirmation:

I acknowledge and celebrate all my achievements this year.

December 22nd

Affirmation:

I am grateful for the challenges that have helped me grow.

December 23rd
Affirmation:
I choose to focus on the positive memories of this year.

December 24th

Affirmation:

I am thankful for the people who have made this year special.

December 25th

Affirmation:

I am grateful for the wisdom and insight I have gained.

December 26th
Affirmation:
I am thankful for the love, joy, and abundance in my life.

December 27th
Affirmation:
I reflect on this year with peace, love, and gratitude.

December 28th

Affirmation:

I am grateful for the opportunities that have helped me grow.

December 29th

Affirmation:

I choose to end this year with gratitude and reflection.

December 30th

Affirmation:

I am thankful for the experiences that have shaped me this year.

December 31st

Affirmation:

I welcome the new year with an open heart, full of hope, gratitude, and endless possibilities.

Also by Asha

The Realm of Echoing Hearts: Adventures Beyond the Veil
The Author's Curse
365 Days of Positivity Quotes